WORKI

MW00887124

For

The Awe of God

*The Astounding Way a Healthy
Fear of God Transforms Your Life*

A Guide For John Bevere's Book

KHAY PRESS

DEAR READER

Disclaimer: This is an independently UNOFFICIAL, UNAUTHORIZED workbook designed to serve as a companion to the original book and enhance your reading experience.

The information presented in this book is based on the author's research and personal experience. Khay Press has not added a different view from what was expressed by the author in the original book. At the same time, the author has made every effort to ensure that the information provided is from a reliable, accurate, and up-to-date source; readers are advised to verify the information before making any decisions or taking any actions based on it.

The author and publisher disclaim any liability whatsoever that may come from the use or misuse of the information contained in this book. The reader is solely responsible for their actions and decisions.

The author intends not to use this book as a substitute for professional advice or treatment. Readers should always consult a qualified professional before making medical, legal, or financial decisions.
This is an unofficial summary and analytical review. It is not affiliated, authorized, approved, or licensed by the subject book's author or publisher.

Contents

Introduction

The term "fear of God" can be quite multifaceted, evoking a range of profound impressions and thoughts. Many individuals automatically associate this term with the image of an all-powerful and strict deity.

This way of thinking often makes people afraid that even asking essential questions about life and existence could make God punish them. Even just thinking about what might happen if you try to learn more can be scary.

However, it is crucial to learn more about what God is like. While some perceive God as a punishing force, the question remains; How can He at the same time show kindness and compassion? This apparent contradiction makes us reconsider what it truly means to fear God.

Author John Bevere made it clear in his book "The Awe of God" that the fear of God is not solely about being terrified for our lives. Rather, it entails recognizing the awe-inspiring majesty and power of a divine being beyond human comprehension. It involves acknowledging the magnitude of God's authority and our limitations in contrast.

In this context, fear is more closely aligned with reverence, respect, and a deep sense of humility.

To fear God might mean approaching Him with awe and humility, acknowledging His sovereignty over all things. It is an acknowledgment that we are finite beings in the presence of the infinite, recognizing our need for guidance, forgiveness, and redemption.

This fear does not stem from paralyzing terror but rather from a desire to cultivate a sincere connection with the divine and align our actions with higher principles.

In essence, the fear of God involves balancing and recognizing God's power and authority with understanding His benevolence and love. By embracing this multifaceted concept, we can strive to deepen our spiritual journey and develop a harmonious relationship with the divine.

This workbook encourages your spiritual development, equips you to live a life by God's awe-inspiring nature, and encourages a deeper relationship with Him as you travel towards greater faith and a more profound knowledge of the fear of God.

It also has thought-provoking questions that will help you gain clarity and prayer points to strengthen your relationship with God.

Suggested 30 Days Bible Reading Plan On Fear Of God

Day 1: Proverbs 1:7	Day 9: Exodus 18:21
Day 2: Proverbs 9:10	Day 10: Exodus 20:20
Day 3: Proverbs 2:1-5	Day 11: 2 Chronicles 19:7
Day 5: Proverbs 19:23	Day 12: Psalms 25:14
Day 6: 2 Samuel 23:3	Day 13: Psalms 34:11
Day 7: Matthew 10:28	Day 14: Luke 1:50
Day 8: Job 28:28	Day 15: 1 Peter 5:6-7

Day 16: Philippians 2:12-13	Day 24: Zephaniah 3:7
Day 17: Deuteronomy 11:22	Day 25: Revelation 11:18
Day 18: Deuteronomy 31:6	Day 26: Psalm 111:5
Day 19: Romans 8:38-39	Day 27: Deuteronomy 14:23
Day 20: Isaiah 6:3-5	Day 28: Psalm 33:8
Day 21: Acts 9:31	Day 29: Proverbs 10:27
Day 22: Nehemiah 1:11	Day 30: Proverbs 15:33
Day 23: Ecclesiastes 8:12-13	

Commitment Statement

_____

_____

_____

_____

_____

_____

_____

_____

_____

_____

_____

_____

_____

What It Means To Fear God

Understanding the concept of fearing God or a higher power goes beyond its surface meaning. The word "fear" can be misleading, as it typically connotes feeling scared or threatened. This makes fear seem like a bad thing to avoid or overcome.

When it comes to the fear of God, on the other hand, there is a more profound and expansive knowledge that has the potential to change and strengthen our lives. This fear is not about trembling in terror before a wrathful deity but is rooted in reverence, awe, and profound respect for the divine.

We embrace this fear and open ourselves to a deeper connection with the divine. It inspires us to acknowledge the greatness, wisdom, and goodness associated with the divine, cultivating a sense of humility and awe in the face of something greater than ourselves.

To effectively harness the transformational power of the fear of God, one must discern between these two types of fear: constructive and destructive.

Constructive fear catalyzes positive change. It compels us to revere and honor a higher power, providing a moral compass that guides our actions and decisions.

When we constructively fear God, we are motivated to align our lives with justice, compassion, and integrity principles. This reverence for the divine enables us to find meaning, purpose, and fulfillment.

On the other hand, destructive fear hinders our progress and stifles personal growth. It is characterized by anxiety, insecurity, and feeling overwhelmed. This fear prevents us from taking risks, pursuing our dreams, and embracing new opportunities.

Recognizing the difference between constructive and destructive fear empowers us to navigate life's challenges effectively. By cultivating constructive fear, we develop resilience, perseverance, and courage. Constructive fear motivates us to overcome obstacles, learn from our mistakes, and continuously strive for personal and spiritual growth.

Conversely, by identifying and combatting destructive fear, we liberate ourselves from self-imposed limitations and embrace a mindset of possibility and abundance. We become more willing to take calculated risks, embrace uncertainty, and pursue our passions wholeheartedly.

In essence, understanding the fear of God in its truest sense allows us to transcend superficial interpretations. It encourages us to approach life with reverence, humility, and a deep connection to something greater than ourselves.

By harnessing the power of constructive fear and rejecting the grip of destructive fear, we can cultivate a fulfilling and purposeful existence characterized by self-awareness, wisdom, emotional intelligence, and a harmonious relationship with the divine.

Reflect on your understanding of the fear of God or a higher power. How has this concept evolved? What does it mean to you now?

_____

_____

_____

_____

_____

_____

How has your knowledge of God's word impacted your understanding of what it means to have the fear of God?

_____

_____

_____

_____

_____

_____

Fear in Your Life:

- Can you recall specific moments in your life where fear had a significant impact on the choices you made and the outcomes that followed?

- Take the time to categorize each instance into either constructive or destructive fear.

- Reflect on the influence each type of fear had on your decision-making process and the results that followed.

Building a Moral Compass:

- Think about the values and principles that guide your actions in life. Reflect on how they align with your beliefs and understanding of the world. Also, consider how embracing the fear of God can help you develop a strong moral compass to guide you through different challenges and situations in life.

- Think about the areas in your life where this guidance could be most helpful. It could provide direction in your personal relationships or professional pursuits or help you overcome daily struggles and challenges. Consider how this advice could be beneficial for you and your specific needs.

It's important to take a moment and reflect on the benefits of incorporating the fear of God into your decision-making process. Doing so can bring greater clarity, purpose, and fulfillment to your life, no matter your circumstances.

Psalm 115:11 made a great promise to those who fear the Lord. What has God revealed to you about "those who fear Him."?

_____

_____

_____

_____

_____

_____

_____

_____

_____

_____

_____

_____

STUDY THE WORD

Today's Scripture:

Reflections

Prayer Point:

Heavenly Father. I pray that You would fill my heart with a reverential fear of Your greatness and holiness.

Lord Teach Me To

STUDY THE WORD

Date:_____

Today's Scripture:

Reflections

Prayer Point:

Lord, help me to always approach You
with awe and respect, acknowledging
Your sovereignty over all things.

Lord Teach Me To

STUDY THE WORD

Date:_____

Today's Scripture:

Reflections

Prayer Point: ✝

Father, forgive me for any times when I have treated Your presence lightly or taken Your love for granted.

Lord Teach Me To

Today's Scripture:

Reflections

Prayer Point:

Holy Spirit, deepen my understanding of Your holiness and ignite in me a burning desire to live a life pleasing to You.

Lord Teach Me To

Date:_____

Today's Scripture:

Reflections

Prayer Point:

Lord, grant me the wisdom to discern between what is holy and what is unholy, and give me the strength to choose what is right in Your sight.

Lord Teach Me To

STUDY THE WORD

Date:_____

Today's Scripture:

Reflections

Prayer Point: ✝

Heavenly Father, teach me to walk in humility before You, recognizing that You alone are deserving of all honor and glory.

Lord Teach Me To

STUDY THE WORD

Date:_____

Today's Scripture:

Reflections

Prayer Point: ✝

Lord Jesus, help me to surrender every aspect of my life to You, knowing that You are worthy of my complete devotion.

Lord Teach Me To

Beyond The Word "Fear"

When we talk about fearing God, it goes beyond a mere sense of being afraid. It encompasses a deep reverence and awe for the divine power. This reverence extends not only to God but also to the life we have been given. It is a consistent attitude of holding God and our existence in high regard.

Reverence helps us realize we are part of something bigger. It reveals the immensity of the universe and our interconnectedness with all life. This helps us understand that our choices have a ripple effect, impacting ourselves and the world around us.

Reverence helps form a moral compass. It inspires us to follow our core values. Integrity and reverence for the divine deepen our relationship to a higher force. This relationship guides and supports personal growth. It gives us the strength and purpose to overcome life's problems.

It's been shown severally that reverence to a higher power makes you feel more grateful, happy, and at peace with yourself. This comes from being grateful for what you have and the feeling that you are part of something bigger than yourself. These good feelings significantly affect mental health and well-being, laying the groundwork for personal growth and change.

In summary, fearing God involves consistent reverence and awe toward the divine and our existence. It fosters an understanding of our interconnectedness with the world and inspires mindful actions.

Reverence has the power to inspire individuals to make positive contributions to their communities and undergo personal transformations.

It helps us develop a strong moral compass, guides us through life's challenges, and brings about psychological benefits such as gratitude, happiness, and inner peace. Through the comprehensive practice of reverence, we embark on a journey of self-discovery, connectedness, and holistic well-being.

How does the concept of reverence for a higher power impact your perspective on life and the actions you take daily?

_____

_____

_____

_____

_____

_____

Think about a challenging situation in your life right now and reflect on how your reverence for God can provide strength and purpose to overcome obstacles.

_____

_____

_____

_____

_____

_____

_____

How does your reverence for the divine help you stay true to your core values and live with integrity? Share experiences from your own life.

_____

_____

_____

_____

_____

_____

_____

_____

_____

_____

_____

_____

Reflect on how having reverence for God can make you happier, more grateful, and more at peace with yourself. Share specific instances where these benefits have manifested in your life.

_____

_____

_____

_____

_____

_____

_____

_____

_____

_____

_____

_____

_____

Personal Growth Blueprint:

- Develop a personal growth plan that incorporates the principles of reverence. You should tailor this plan toward your specific needs and goals. Start by reflecting on what reverence means to you and how it can help your growth journey.

- Consider how you can strengthen your connection to a higher power, whether that is through prayer, meditation, or attending religious services.

Reviewing and making changes to your personal growth plan should be done on a regular basis. This will help you keep going toward your goals and stay on track.

Recognizing Interconnectedness:

- Consider how viewing yourself as a part of a larger, interconnected community can affect your daily actions.

- When you think about contributing positively to your community, how does that align with the concept of fearing God? Understanding how your actions affect the community and the world is essential.

- Consider taking specific actions to have a positive impact. This could be anything from volunteering, donating, or being compassionate to those around you.

When you recognize your place in the larger community and how your actions can affect others, you can work towards making a positive difference in the world.

STUDY THE WORD

Date:_____

Today's Scripture:

Reflections

Prayer Point:

Lord, may the holy fear of You shape every aspect of my life, leading me into deeper intimacy with You and ultimately bringing glory to Your name.

Lord Teach Me To

| |
| |
| |
| |
| |
| |

STUDY THE WORD

Date:_____

Today's Scripture:

Reflections

Prayer Point:

Holy Spirit, guide me in making decisions that honor You and align with Your plans for my life, even if they go against the ways of the world.

Lord Teach Me To

STUDY THE WORD

Date:_____

Today's Scripture:

Reflections

Prayer Point:

Father, grant me a heart that is quick to forgive and show mercy, just as You have forgiven and shown mercy to me.

Lord Teach Me To

STUDY THE WORD

Date:_____

Today's Scripture:

Reflections

Prayer Point:

Lord Jesus, reveal to me any idols or worldly attachments that have taken priority over my devotion to You and enable me to let go of them.

Lord Teach Me To

STUDY THE WORD

Date:_____

Today's Scripture:

Reflections

Prayer Point:

Heavenly Father, release me from any bondage to fear or anxiety and help me to trust in Your unfailing love and faithfulness.

Lord Teach Me To

STUDY THE WORD

Date:_____

Today's Scripture:

Reflections

Prayer Point: ✝

Lord, fill me with a deep love for Your Word and a hunger to study and apply it daily, so that I may grow in wisdom and understanding.

Lord Teach Me To

STUDY THE WORD

Today's Scripture:

Reflections

Prayer Point:

Father, protect me from the fear of man and help me to fear You alone, for You hold my present and my future in Your hands.

Lord Teach Me To

Humility: The Seed Of Holy Fear

One of the things constructive fear of God can help us do is to be humble. Humility helps us acknowledge our limitations and become more open to the wisdom and guidance of a higher power.

Embracing humility can help us in the following ways:

Personal Growth: Humility acts as a driving force for personal growth and development. When we approach life humbly, we acknowledge that we don't have all the answers and recognize our limitations. This self-awareness opens us up to learning opportunities, allowing us to acquire new knowledge, skills, and perspectives. Embracing humility enables us to continuously improve ourselves and strive for excellence without arrogance or complacency.

Meaningful Relationships: Humility is pivotal in fostering meaningful connections with others. When humble, we genuinely listen to others, value their opinions, and appreciate their unique experiences. By setting aside our ego and being open to different viewpoints, we create an environment of respect and understanding, nurturing authentic relationships based on empathy, trust, and mutual growth.

Spiritual Connection: A sense of humility often intertwines with our spiritual beliefs.

Recognizing a higher power or divine presence reminds us that we are part of something greater than ourselves.

Humility allows us to approach spirituality with reverence and awe, acknowledging our dependence on divine wisdom and guidance. It cultivates a deeper connection with our spiritual beliefs and values, providing solace, purpose, and direction.

Resilience: Humility helps us develop resilience in facing challenges and setbacks. When we embrace humility, we accept that failure and adversity are inevitable parts of the journey toward success.

Rather than becoming disheartened or giving up, humility encourages us to learn from our mistakes, adapt our strategies, and persevere with patience and determination. It reminds us that we are constantly growing and evolving, and each obstacle is an opportunity for growth.

Collaboration and Leadership: In collaborative settings, humility is essential for effective teamwork and leadership. A humble leader recognizes the strengths and contributions of others, encourages open communication, and values diverse perspectives.

Such a leader fosters an inclusive environment where team members feel valued and empowered, resulting in increased creativity, productivity, and collaboration.

Compassion and Empathy: Humility enhances our capacity for compassion and empathy. When we are humble, we recognize our shared humanity and interconnectedness.

This understanding cultivates empathy towards others, allowing us to relate to their struggles, joys, and experiences. Humility enables us to treat others with kindness, respect, and understanding, promoting harmony and cooperation within communities and society.

In summary, humility is a vital quality that contributes to personal growth, meaningful relationships, resilience, effective leadership, and compassionate living.

It allows us to embrace our limitations, learn from others, and foster a sense of connectedness with the world around us. By cultivating humility, we can lead more fulfilling lives and positively impact those around us.

Reflect on Personal Humility:

- Have you ever considered the role that humility has played in your life?

Take a moment to reflect on specific instances where approaching situations with a humble mindset has had an impact on your actions and relationships.

Consider how humility has helped you learn from others, resolve conflicts, and strengthen connections with those around you.

- Are there any areas of your life where you could work on cultivating more humility? Perhaps it's in listening more actively to others, accepting feedback graciously, or recognizing your own limitations.

Take some time to write about your experiences with humility and how you can continue to foster this quality in yourself.

_____

_____

_____

_____

_____

Learning from Failures:

The exercise requires you to reflect on a time(s) when you faced a setback or failure in your life. The goal is to explore how embracing humility can transform such experiences into valuable learning opportunities.

To gain more insight, you might think about the multi-billionaire's experience, which John shared in the original book, who recognized failure as a necessary component of his path to success.

When facing obstacles, it's important to develop a mindset of humility and trust in the process, even when the path forward seems uncertain.

By adopting this approach, you can learn from your mistakes, grow as an individual, and ultimately achieve your goals. It's important to come up with solid strategies that will help you deal with problems in this way every time.

Give an example of a humble person(s) you respect. How do they show humility? What specific things do they do or have that make them humble? How does the person(s) inspire you and others with their humility?

_____

_____

_____

_____

_____

_____

_____

_____

_____

_____

_____

_____

_____

_____

Reflect on your support system. How can humility play a role in acknowledging that you don't have all the answers? Identify individuals or resources that can contribute to your personal and professional growth.

_____

_____

_____

_____

_____

_____

_____

_____

_____

_____

_____

_____

_____

How has humility influenced your willingness to acknowledge limitations and trust the process of seeking divine guidance? What changes have you observed in your mindset and decision-making?

_____

_____

_____

_____

_____

_____

_____

_____

_____

_____

_____

_____

_____

STUDY THE WORD

Date:_____

Today's Scripture:

Reflections

Prayer Point:

Holy Spirit, empower me to resist temptation and flee from anything that leads me away from a holy and righteous life.

Lord Teach Me To

STUDY THE WORD

Date:_____

Today's Scripture:

Prayer Point:

Lord Jesus, help me walk in integrity and honesty, knowing that my actions reflect my reverence for You.

Lord Teach Me To

STUDY THE WORD

Date:_____

Today's Scripture:

Reflections

Prayer Point:

Heavenly Father, grant me the courage to stand firm in my faith and not compromise my beliefs, even in the face of opposition or persecution.

Lord Teach Me To

STUDY THE WORD

Date:_____

Today's Scripture:

Prayer Point:

Father, grant me a spirit of humility that acknowledges my dependence on You and seeks Your guidance and direction in all things.

Lord Teach Me To

STUDY THE WORD

Date:_____

Today's Scripture:

Reflections

Prayer Point:

Lord Jesus, instill in me a deep reverence for the sacredness of marriage, family, and relationships, and protect them from any form of sin or harm.

Lord Teach Me To

STUDY THE WORD

Date:_____

Today's Scripture:

Reflections

Prayer Point:

Heavenly Father, guard my tongue from speaking words that dishonor You or hurt others, and help me to use my words to build up and encourage.

Lord Teach Me To

STUDY THE WORD

Date:_____

Today's Scripture:

Reflections

Prayer Point:

Father, give me discernment to recognize false teachings and ideologies that try to diminish Your holiness and authority.

Lord Teach Me To

Wisdom To Build A Legacy

The connection between the fear of God and wisdom may seem counterintuitive at first. However, examining it closely, we realize this fear is not about dread or terror but rather reverential awe and deep respect for a higher power. It is an acknowledgment of our limitations as human beings and an understanding that greater forces are at play in the universe.

This constructive fear prompts introspection and self-reflection. It compels us to examine our actions, motivations, and beliefs in light of divine principles.

By recognizing our fallibility and seeking guidance from a higher authority, we open ourselves up to learning and growing in wisdom. This humility lets us approach life with grace, empathy, and discernment.

The example given by the author of Max Jukes and Jonathan Edwards's families further illustrates the transformative power of the fear of God.

Max Jukes' family tree reveals a lineage of crime, dysfunction, and reliance on government support. In contrast, Jonathan Edwards' descendants include notable figures who have contributed significantly in various fields.

What distinguished these families was the presence of a fear of God in the life of Jonathan Edwards, his wife, and their children. Their devotion to faith and the principles they instilled in their children led to lives characterized by wisdom, purpose, and positive impact.

Also, having a constructive fear of God can help us better understand our place in the world. When we think about how big the world is, how complicated nature is, and how everything is linked, we understand how complicated life is. This broader view motivates us to seek wisdom, learn as much as possible, and get a complete picture of the world.

Wisdom gained through the fear of God enables us to make better decisions and navigate life's challenges with integrity, compassion, and humility. It helps us distinguish between right and wrong, discern the true nature of things, and act following higher principles and values.
This wisdom extends to our relationships, work, and every aspect of our lives, allowing us to lead a more purposeful and fulfilling existence.

It is important to note that the fear of God encourages a healthy reverence that motivates us to seek truth, pursue knowledge, and align our actions with universal principles such as love, justice, and compassion. It invites us to engage in a lifelong growth, learning, and self-improvement journey.

Reflect on the role that one's upbringing and the family they were raised play in forming one's values and ideas. In what ways does the fear of God, or the lack thereof, play a role in the dynamics of your own family life or the lives of those around you?

Identify key decisions made by family members based on their faith. Reflect on how these decisions shaped the family's collective wisdom and legacy.

_____

_____

_____

_____

_____

_____

_____

_____

_____

_____

_____

The teachings of the main book practically show us that fear of God doesn't mean being terrified and avoiding Him; rather, it means building a deep relationship that will bring us closer to God. What steps are you taking to build a close relationship with Him?

_____

_____

_____

_____

_____

_____

_____

_____

_____

_____

_____

_____

Some people believe that wisdom stems from a deep reverence for God, while others argue that it's the opposite. In my opinion, separating the two is difficult because they are closely intertwined. By fearing God, we consciously submit to His dominion and acknowledge His absolute control over our existence.

When we embrace humility, we create an opportunity for personal growth and the acquisition of knowledge. When we seek wisdom, we often realize how little we know and how much we need God's guidance.

By recognizing this, our reverence and sense of awe for God can grow stronger. Therefore, we can observe a beautiful and meaningful connection between fearing God and wisdom.

What is your understanding of the connection between fearing God and wisdom?

_____

_____

_____

_____

_____

_____

STUDY THE WORD

Date:_____

Today's Scripture:

Reflections

Prayer Point:

Father, protect me from the snares of sin and deliver me from any attitudes or behaviors that dishonor Your name.

Lord Teach Me To

STUDY THE WORD

Date:_____

Today's Scripture:

Reflections

Prayer Point:

Holy Spirit, convict me whenever I stray from the path of righteousness and draw me back into a deeper relationship with You.

Lord Teach Me To

STUDY THE WORD

Date:_____

Today's Scripture:

Reflections

Prayer Point:

Lord, purify my heart and cleanse me from all unrighteousness, so that I may be a vessel fit for Your use.

Lord Teach Me To

STUDY THE WORD

Date:_____

Today's Scripture:

Prayer Point:

Lord Jesus, help me to understand the gravity of my sins and the immense price You paid for my redemption on the cross.

Lord Teach Me To

STUDY THE WORD

Today's Scripture:

Reflections

Prayer Point:

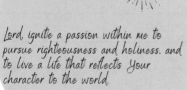

Lord, ignite a passion within me to pursue righteousness and holiness, and to live a life that reflects Your character to the world.

Lord Teach Me To

STUDY THE WORD

Date:_____

Today's Scripture:

Reflections

Prayer Point:

Lord, give me a heart that trembles at Your Word and delights in meditating on it day and night.

Lord Teach Me To

STUDY THE WORD

Date:_____

Today's Scripture:

Reflections

Prayer Point:

Holy Spirit, convict me of any hidden sins or areas of compromise in my life, and lead me towards repentance and restoration.

Lord Teach Me To

Fear Of God Helps Us Deal With Issues

Getting to know God on a deep and personal level is a powerful and life-changing journey that can significantly affect our lives. It means building a relationship with a greater power, which you can do with a constructive fear of God.

This fear is not a sign of terror or worry but of respectful awe and respect for the presence of God. By having this attitude, we create an atmosphere that helps us grow spiritually and improves our connection to God.

When we approach our relationship with the divine in this manner, it becomes easier to lead a more authentic and fulfilling existence.

Our connection to a higher power provides guidance, purpose, and a sense of belonging. It allows us to align our actions and decisions with our values and beliefs, enabling us to live in harmony with ourselves and the world around us.

In the context of personal relationships, having a mutual understanding and respect for a higher power can contribute to the growth of these relationships.

John passionately spoke about the unwavering strength of his relationship with his wife, Lisa, attributing it to their shared belief in God. Their shared spiritual beliefs give them a solid basis for their relationship.

It encourages honest and open dialogue, mutual respect, and a strong commitment to the relationship. Keeping their spiritual link strong made it easy for them to grow closer and understand each other better.

Keeping a close relationship with the divine also promotes self-reflection and introspection. It makes us think about our principles and values and how we live by them daily.

The self-awareness we get by reflecting on our connection to God empowers us to live authentically, aligning our thoughts, actions, and relationships with our core values and principles.

A strong connection with God gives us stability and comfort when life gets hard. When we feel like a greater power supports and guides us, we can better handle challenging situations with grace and strength. This link gives us a strong faith that doesn't waver.

This faith can be like an anchor, keeping us rooted when things go wrong. It provides us with the strength and courage to stick with things, learn from them, and grow from them.

In short, if we want a close and deep relationship with God, building a healthy fear of God is crucial, and creating an environment that helps our spiritual growth. This connection is the basis for living a real and satisfying life, alone and with others.

By reflecting on our beliefs and values, we gain self-awareness and live in alignment with our true selves. Ultimately, our strong bond with the divine provides us with stability, guidance, and resilience, enabling us to face life's challenges with strength and perseverance.

Going forward, what approach will you adopt when it comes to your prayer life and understanding of His Word?

_____

_____

_____

_____

_____

_____

_____

_____

_____

_____

_____

_____

_____

Do you think God is pleased with the way you live your life? How can you adjust your conduct to live a life that's pleasing to God?

_____

_____

_____

_____

_____

_____

_____

_____

_____

_____

_____

_____

_____

Take some time to think about any concerns or worries regarding your faith or relationship with God. In what ways could having a reverent fear of God make it easier to face and conquer these worries?

_____

_____

_____

_____

_____

_____

_____

_____

_____

_____

_____

_____

_____

STUDY THE WORD

Date:_____

Today's Scripture:

Reflections

Prayer Point:

Holy Spirit, empower me to live a life that reflects Your holiness, so that others may see Your light shining through me.

Lord Teach Me To

STUDY THE WORD

Date:_____

Today's Scripture:

Reflections

Prayer Point:

Heavenly Father, grant me a spirit of obedience, that I may willingly submit to Your will and follow Your commandments.

Lord Teach Me To

Strong Moral Compass Is Vital

In the book "The Awe of God," John Bevere emphasizes the importance of having a strong moral compass to lead a fulfilling and purposeful life. This moral compass, anchored in the constructive fear of God, serves as a foundation that enables us to navigate life's complexities with gratitude, wisdom, and growth.

Amidst life's chaos, the book underscores the significance of embracing a constructive fear of God. This fear, far from being restrictive, becomes a source of gratitude for the life we lead. Continuous reverence creates a strong moral compass that guides us to knowledge, growth, and happiness.

Justin's story is a powerful illustration that leaves a lasting impression. Being John's employee, Justin shared a close bond with him, which made their relationship more than just professional. Justin struggled and became resistant to correction.

However, three months later, he sought forgiveness, attributing his transformation to the fear of God. This fear became the driving force behind his decision to reevaluate his moral compass, ultimately leading to a newfound respect for those around him.

A clear moral compass gives us the strength to face challenges, stick to our core values, and live a life of honesty, authenticity, and purpose. This gives rise to natural outcomes, such as feeling a deep sense of connection to our fellow human beings, showing kindness and compassion to others, and forming authentic and meaningful relationships.

A strong moral compass helps you make choices and maintain inner peace, making the path to knowledge and happiness easier to take and more satisfying.

"The Awe of God" demonstrates that a life anchored in a well-defined moral compass is worth living. It inspires readers to embrace this perspective, which fosters a sense of gratitude, wisdom, and growth and leads to a life of authenticity, purpose, and inner peace.

Vision Board for Authentic Living:

- Create a vision board representing the life you aspire to lead based on your values and moral compass. Include images and words that symbolize authenticity, integrity, and purpose.

- How does your vision board reflect the key elements of a life led by a strong moral compass?

_____

_____

_____

_____

_____

What steps can you take to bring the vision board's essence into your daily actions and decisions?

_____

_____

_____

_____

_____

Daily Moral Audit:

- At the end of each day, review your actions and decisions. Assess how well they align with your moral compass. Identify areas for improvement and set intentions for the following day.

Values Clarification:

- Take time to identify and list your core values and principles. Reflect on how these values contribute to the person you want to be.

- How do your identified values align with the idea of having a strong moral compass?

_____

_____

_____

_____

In what situations have your values influenced your decisions positively or negatively?

_____

_____

_____

_____

Finishing Strong With God

In today's fast-paced and highly distracting world, moments of stillness and introspection have become increasingly essential for our overall well-being. Whether surrounded by our loved ones in the comfort of our homes or immersed in the busy corporate environment, taking the time to reflect with a sense of holy fear can profoundly impact our lives.

Cultivating a deep connection with a higher power by deliberately creating quiet and contemplative moments allows you to find inner peace, clarity, and direction amidst your daily challenges and pressures. This state of inner peace enhances your productivity and contributes to a more harmonious life.

Also, practicing self-reflection opens doors to personal growth and self-discovery. We can learn much about who we are by looking at our thoughts, feelings, and behaviors in light of our relationship with the divine.

This heightened self-awareness enables us to identify areas for improvement, make necessary changes, and align our lives with our authentic values and purpose. Through this journey of self-discovery guided by our reverence for the divine, we empower ourselves to live more fulfilling, meaningful, and purpose-driven lives.

In addition to personal growth, reflection makes us emotionally strong and gives us the tools to handle life's obstacles with poise and grace. We build mental strength and flexibility by getting to know ourselves well and feeling connected to a greater power.

This lets us adapt and respond well to situations that are constantly changing. It also helps us overcome setbacks, deal with stress, and keep a good attitude even when things don't go our way. In the end, practicing self-reflection and meditation with fear of God in mind has many positive effects on our lives. It makes us feel better, helps our personal growth, makes us more emotionally strong, and brings us closer to God.

These times of introspection help us achieve a greater sense of personal happiness and contentment, bringing us one step closer to reaching our higher potential.

So, armed with an understanding of what it truly means to fear God, we are encouraged to embark on this transformative journey at any time. The blueprint for our personal transformation already resides within us, waiting to be explored and actualized.

By embracing this practice of reflection and committing ourselves to its principles, we can unlock profound spiritual insights, experience personal evolution, and live a life that is aligned with our deepest values and purpose.

Conclusion

In wrapping up the "Workbook For Awe Of God," think of it as a helpful guide that explains big ideas from John Bevere's book, "The Awe of God." This workbook helps turn the idea of fear of God into something incredible—a feeling of awe and respect.

We learned that this awe of God can unlock our hidden abilities. It's like a secret power source for being wise, humble and understanding our feelings better. It pushes us to be real and live with a clear purpose, following a path that feels right with help from something divine.

We connect deeply with something bigger than us by embracing this special awe. It's like having a compass that points us towards doing the right things and living a life that feels true. Regularly looking at ourselves helps us become more challenging, find peace, and know who we are. This helps us grow personally and light up the world around us.

So, as we finish this journey through this workbook, let's hold on to this amazing awe of God. It's not something scary but a cool source of inspiration. It helps us grow and makes a significant impact on the world.

The wisdom from this workbook can guide you to live an authentic, purposeful life filled with awe. It's much more awesome than mere fear. Let's leave a mark on the story of our lives!

Thank You For Reading

Did you enjoy reading this book? Looking for more insightful reads?

Why settle for one when you can explore more?

Check out our other titles and discover your next companion book for your favorite book today by scanning the QR code below

We appreciate your support.

Personal Notes

Personal Notes

Personal Notes

Personal Notes

Made in the USA
Thornton, CO
08/19/24 11:31:34

7fc1eb94-8beb-4923-9849-5911e9c0dd21R01